Shadow Work

Book 2

Facing & Embracing

the Dark Side of Your Soul

By

Kelly Wallace

Professional Psychic Counselor

DrKellyPsychic.com[1]

---

1. http://DrKellyPsychic.com/

Table of Contents

Books by Kelly Wallace

10 Minutes A Day to A Powerful New Life

Become Your Higher Self – Using Spiritual Energy to Transform Your Life

Breaking The Worry Habit – Stop Your Anxious Thoughts And Start Living!

Chakras – Heal, Clear, And Strengthen Your Energy Centers

Clear Your Karma – The Healing Power of Your Past Lives

Contacting Your Spirit Guides – Meeting and Working with Your Invisible Helpers

Creating A Charmed Life – Enchantments to Attract, Repel, Cleanse & Heal

Dream Work – Using The Wisdom Of Your Sleeping Mind To Change Your Waking Life

Energy Work – Heal, Cleanse, and Strengthen Your Aura

Everyday Miracles – Powerful Steps to Wonderful Experiences

Finding Your Life Purpose – Uncover Your Soul's True Goals

Healing the Child Within – Rewrite Your Early Childhood Life Script

How to Cure Candida – Yeast Infection Symptoms, Causes, Diet & Natural Remedies

Spirits I Have Known – Haunted Places, Haunted People

Spiritual Alchemy – Transform Your Life and Everyone In It

The Art Of Happiness – Living A Life Of Peace And Simplicity

The Love You Deserve – Release Toxic Relationships and Attract Your Soulmate

The Mended Soul – Healing Your Mind, Body, & Spirit From Anxiety & Depression

The Overwhelmed Empath – A Guide For Sensitive Souls

The Power of Pets – How to Psychically Communicate with Your Pet

Transforming Your Money Mindset – From Broke To Abundance

True Wealth – Reprogram Your Subconscious for Financial Success

Upgrade Your Life – Small Changes, Easy Actions, Big Success

Way Of The Lightworker – Discovering Your Role & Following Your Path

Working With Your Angels – Contact Your Loving Guardians

About Kelly Wallace

Kelly is a bestselling spiritual and self-help author, former radio show host, and has been a professional psychic counselor for over twenty years. She can see, hear, sense, and feel information sent from Spirit, the Universe, and a client's Higher Self.

Whether your problems or concerns center on love, finances, family, career, health, education, or your purpose in life, she writes books that will help you easily make lasting changes.

Kelly also offers professional psychic counseling, caring guidance, and solutions that work! More than just a typical psychic reading or counseling session, you will feel you've found a real friend during your time of need—whether you simply want answers and guidance to your current worries or concerns, or you're interested in learning more about your soulmate, spirit guides, angels, past lives, or anything else.

Contact her today for an in-depth and life-altering reading!

Website: DrKellyPsychic.com[1]

---

1. http://psychicreadingsbydrkelly.webs.com/

Email: Dr.Kelly.Psychic.Counselor@gmail.com

What This Book Covers

The Journey Continues

My first book on this subject, *Shadow Work – Understanding and Making Peace With Your Darker Side,* quickly became my best seller. This told me a few things: One, there's been a huge shift in the way the world thinks. People are more open to exploring themselves at a far deeper level than before. Two, people are learning that even those dark parts of themselves really aren't bad at all and can ultimately be helpful.

Where there's light, there are shadows. Turning your back on your shadow doesn't make it disappear. It's still there and always will be. It's far better to face it and embrace it. In doing so, you'll find the healing, power, and freedom you've been searching for.

In this book, *Advanced Shadow Work – Facing and Embracing The Dark Side of Your Soul* we'll dig in deeper, cover more ground, and do more work that leads to ultimate healing and freedom. I'll show you how to view your shadow traits differently, integrate them, and use them as a powerful force that can help you in life rather than holding you back.

Your shadow self, those darker aspects of your personality, are ones you've spent years, perhaps decades, hiding from. In polite society, we're taught to only show those nice parts of ourselves to the outside world. We should be kind, generous, thoughtful, calm, and always smiling. Those areas of us that we worry people won't accept—the anger, fear, selfishness, laziness, loudness, and sadness—gets pushed into the shadows.

The more you stuff in there, the bigger this darker part becomes. If you don't work through it and eventually accept it and get it to work for you rather than against you, it's going to make you miserable in more than one way. Your shadow won't stay hidden. It's not possible because, after all, it's part of you. It will show up again and again as emotional outbursts or chronic problems with money, love, and/or your health.

Some people think that only those with messed up childhoods or who have gone through traumatic things in life have a shadow. *Everyone has one.* Because, no matter how positive and healthy your childhood was, somewhere along the way you felt deprived of something, felt powerless, or unaccepted. These were the beginnings of your shadow self.

Maybe you threw a tantrum or took a toy away from another child when you were young and your parents scolded you. At that moment you learned that if you show those parts of yourself—such as anger or envy or greed—it made you less lovable. The way you acted wasn't acceptable to the people who you trusted to keep you safe and to love you unconditionally.

You then became fragmented and no longer a whole person. You learned that there are good parts of yourself and bad parts. The bad ones get hidden each time they emerge until you're ultimately consumed by your shadow or forced to make peace with it once and for all.

When you look at it this way, it seems like we *should* suppress our shadow side. After all, who doesn't want to be loved, liked, and appreciated? However, those wounded parts of us that have been stuffed down are the path to becoming your authentic self and living a fulfilling life.

Before you can heal and grow though, you'll need to do shadow work. Not to necessarily fix what's broken, but to shed light on those dark parts and understand every aspect of who you truly are. Eventually, by embracing those less-than-perfect aspects of your personality, it will lead you to freedom.

I'll be honest, Shadow Work is not easy, nor is it an overnight fix. Many give up before even starting or after doing very little work. It can be overwhelming when faced with all of your demons and dirty laundry, so to speak. Exploring all of those wounded and dark parts of you can make you feel worse in the beginning.

That's why I wrote these books though. I don't want you to go down this road alone. I've been doing my own shadow work for years, and have helped many clients through their journey as well. Let me walk with you as you face and embrace your shadows.

Everyone Has A Shadow

I've often heard people say, "I'm a good person! There's no way that I have a shadow side!" I get it, believing that the opposite of all your good traits is living inside you makes you feel uneasy. I felt that way myself.

But another truth is that everything within you, within us all, and in all of the Universe is in balance. You can't know love without knowing hate. You can't know happiness without experiencing sadness, or vibrant health without having been ill. And, just as we all prefer to project our light out into the world, there's darkness in everyone.

This darkness was created by our childhood conditioning. I'd even go so far as to say that it's shaped by past lives as well, but I cover the subject of past lives, karma, and other topics in my book *Clear Your Karma – The Healing Power Of Past Lives*. For simplicity's sake, we're going to focus on your present life since it's the one that matters most at this time.

Even if you volunteer at a soup kitchen, donate to charity, or do many other selfless things, the fact is, you're human and every human has both a light and dark side, and we prefer to deny the darkness in us. Rather than fighting against it or pretending it doesn't exist, you need to understand and work with it instead.

Okay, so you know you have a shadow side and perhaps you've already been doing some shadow work, or perhaps you're just about to embark on the journey. Although this book is on advanced shadow work, anyone can jump in and start or continue. Yes, it's hard work and takes time, so what are the real benefits of putting yourself through this lengthy healing process?

1. You'll learn to love and accept all facets of yourself and become whole.

2. You'll have better and closer relationships with friends, family, and your partner.

3. You'll be your authentic self at long last and feel far more confident and happier.

4. You'll gain mental, emotional, and spiritual peace and clarity.

5. Your mental and physical health will improve.

6. You'll understand others better and have more compassion and empathy.

7. Your creativity will expand as you discover hidden talents.

8. Your natural gifts of intuition will become stronger and more reliable.

9. You'll reach goals you've put off or failed at before.

10. You'll find more meaning in life, your purpose in life, and enjoy life far more.

11. You'll go with the flow of things rather than needing control or fearing change.

12. You'll achieve things in life that have always been difficult or out of reach.

13. You'll feel whole and complete at long last.

This list could be much longer, but these are just some of the wonderful benefits that come along with shadow work. Will it happen right away? No. Nothing about this path is quick, though you'll probably find that many things that used to bother you or create obstacles in your life start to fade very soon. The key is to not give up and to always stay the course. Persistence pays! Very soon, your life will be blessed far more than you can currently imagine.

Honesty Is A Must

When you're honest with yourself and accept your shadow traits it allows you to grow beyond them and realize that you are not these "good" or "bad" things, but that they're merely thoughts and feelings that come and go. Only when we allow them to consume us or dictate our lives does the shadow hold us back. And yet, the bigger and louder those dark elements become, the more we need to pay attention and work on them.

What usually happens though is we feel an uncomfortable emotion rising to the surface and the first thing we want to do is deny it.

- "I'm not a jealous person so why am I having these negative feelings about my friend who just bought a new car?"

- "I'm not an angry person so when my partner forgot my birthday why did I give them the silent treatment or lash out?"

- "I'm not normally insecure, so why do I not like that new person in our department who seems to be kissing up to the boss?"

Denying these feelings, ignoring them, or, worse yet, being blind to them and simply acting on them, puts your shadow in the driver's seat. You can't learn from or get beyond these darker feelings until you admit to yourself that you actually do possess them in the first place. The next step is being honest with yourself as to why you feel this way now and what might have sparked these feelings initially in your past. We'll cover ways to do that later on in this book.

An easy way to know where your shadows take up residence is this: Pay attention to your thoughts every time you judge or condemn others because, in truth, that means you're simply looking back into yourself and the things you don't like there. To be a whole person you need to acknowledge, accept, and ultimately be at peace with all facets of your personality.

That doesn't mean that when a darker aspect of who you are rears its head that you should just ride along with it. Instead, it's about being mindful and honest that, just as love and compassion exist within you, so does hate and indifference.

Accepting these "less acceptable" parts of yourself is different than some spiritual methods teach. They tell you to have more discipline against these dark traits or to repress them and they'll eventually go away. That's just not possible and incredibly unrealistic.

Let's say you have a cut on your hand and you ignore it. The cut gets infected and is painful, yet you still ignore it. Soon, the infection spreads and the pain is nearly unbearable. So, do you have your hand amputated? No, you tend to the wound, apply the proper treatment, and soon it heals.

In society and nearly all relationships, this seems completely unacceptable though. We're taught from birth to wear a false mask and to squash down and never explore those very real yet incredibly messy aspects of our personalities.

At the opposite end of the spectrum, I've met people who solely operate from their shadow side. They're perpetually angry, argumentative, egotistical, hardhearted, rude, or greedy. These people are afraid of appearing weak so they wear their shadow like a suit of impenetrable armor.

To be your authentic self, a whole person, and experience true self-love and growth you need to take a good look at each of your shadow traits and be honest. Going down into that darkness and seeing what lies there beneath the muck and mire isn't easy, but necessary.

When we look into the shadow and see everything lurking there it's hard to believe that we'd want to face all of that stuff, let alone embrace it. But in reality, those very real parts of you are actually empowering.

Side Effects Of The Shadow

Most people are unaware that they have a shadow side while others know about it but choose to ignore it or don't know what to do about it. If you haven't made a conscious effort to acknowledge, work with, and integrate your shadow, you'll find one or more of these common side effects running through your life.

1. Difficulty in relationships.

This can be friendships, family, or coworkers, though the shadow self is biggest when it comes to intimate partnerships. We find ourselves attracting the same type of dysfunctional romantic partners and friendships, arguing or feeling cut-off from family members, and a whole host of other problems.

All of this truly feels like it's out of our hands because we're trying so hard to do things differently, and yet subconsciously we're being led around by the shadow self. In truth, we attract what we need to work on most within ourselves.

2. Feeling like an outsider, distant from others, or isolated.

If you're an empath and/or pursuing your spirituality, it's easy to feel that you're traveling your path alone. What I'm talking about here though is different. When we ignore those darker sides of ourselves it not only cuts us off from being whole as a spirit and human but it severs us from everyone around us as well.

We feel nobody understands, nobody gets us, or we simply don't mesh with others. In truth, it's that you're disconnected internally and there's no way to feel that you belong unless you mend yourself first.

3. Repeating patterns.

Whether it comes to money, love, health, or any other goal, you encounter the same setbacks and obstacles again and again. It doesn't matter if you feel you're doing things differently or you believe you've finally found someone different. It doesn't matter if you found a better-paying job or won the lottery.

If you haven't worked on your shadow self the outcome will always be the same as it has been. Very often, it might even be worse because your shadow is trying to get your attention and will try harder and get louder until you do.

4. Exhibiting "dark" behaviors.

You see yourself as a good person and try to act accordingly, yet you sometimes get angry, jealous, manipulative, needy, insecure, or weak. Someone cuts you off while you're driving, you feel your temper shoot to the surface, and you curse at the person. You see your significant other talking to someone you don't know and insecurity and suspicion rise up. Later, you give them the silent treatment or erupt and spew angry accusations.

Afterward, you might feel shocked or embarrassed, wondering why you would do those things when you're clearly not like that at all. Or maybe you believe you're justified in feeling and acting the way you do, though, in the long run, it gets you nowhere and only makes your shadow bigger.

5. Feelings of low energy and apathy.

Everyone around you seems to have passion and drive. They have goals they're working toward, successes they're building on, and lives that they're making happier every day. You don't know how they do it because you can't summon the energy to do more than just get through the day and crawl into bed at night.

You've tried finding something, anything, anyone, that would have you feeling energized and excited, but nothing works. It's not that you're clinically depressed, it's just a constant low-level feeling of indifference or numbness. This is because you're shadow is casting its darkness onto any possible light in your life.

After reading all of that I'm sure you can see times where you've felt and acted in these ways. No, it's not flattering, and most of the time it feels awful. It's hard to believe that doing shadow work can help you to heal and conquer all these things I've talked about and more, but I'm living proof that it's true. Once you start addressing each of your shadow traits you just might be surprised at how much better you feel and how life starts moving along more smoothly.

It's Bigger Than You Think

If you read my first book on shadow work and have already done the exercises, you know it's not easy, though necessary to living life as your authentic self. As we cover more territory in this book, you might find yourself wanting to take a step back or give up altogether. It can be exhausting because our shadow selves are bigger than we think they are.

Everything you've suppressed in life or labeled as "bad" was sent to your shadow for a reason. You put these behaviors there because someone told you, or you discovered for yourself, that acting and reacting in such a way is negative. You wanted to be loved, you wanted to feel safe, you wanted to be happy, and anything you did that could prevent that was shoved way down. You learned to behave in the way that the outside world would find acceptable.

Let's say that you grew up with siblings. It's natural for kids, especially the sensitive ones, to suppress the parts of themselves that they see as less lovable. They want to know that they're loved just as much as their siblings are. They want to earn their place in the family and not demand too much.

Almost always, these fears aren't real though. Most parents wouldn't disown their child for misbehaving or not being perfect. Children don't have mature, rational minds though, and worrying about how much their parents love them is a big worry for so many kids.

I was like this for far too many years. I had only one sister, four years younger than me, who got all the attention and praise. It wasn't her fault, it's just how differently my parents treated us. So, how could I be special too? In my mind, if I was always agreeable, always helpful, always took care of others, I would have my place in the family and prove myself valuable.

As you can imagine, this became ingrained in me and created a lot of stress and resentment over the years. I knew that those feelings were "bad" so they were pushed aside and became part of my shadow self. For decades my shadow grew until I was forced to face it and work *with* it rather than against it.

It's hard knowing what parts of us need healing and it's difficult to see just how free we would feel once we do shadow work. For so long you've put up a barrier that kept you safe from those painful memories. You padded on layer after layer of protection so you wouldn't have to deal with the anger, sadness, self-rejection, and a long list of other negative feelings.

Looking into your own shadow is difficult because everything in it is what you've been avoiding for so many years. If you didn't like a certain feeling or a way you acted, then you hid it away in your shadow. Imagine how much is stuffed in there! That's why shadow work takes so much courage. You didn't want to face one episode or another when it first came up, yet now you need to face it all if you want to make peace with your darker side.

Most of us look at our shadow as something to fear or to keep hidden. Instead, we should look at it as an ally, something that's protected us for so long. But now it's time to be honest and have it work with you. Your shadow is so used to doing its job though that it won't give in without a fight.

Shadow Thoughts

We know what types of things are in the shadow, but those are actually far fewer than the infinite number of thoughts that created it and continue to keep adding to it. Catching yourself when you're thinking certain things is one of the first steps to becoming whole. As you'll see from the list, this is just a small example, and the thoughts vary from highly egotistical to extreme insecurity and doubt. These are some of the things we tell ourselves:

1. My past was worse than others

2. My pain is worse than others

3. I'm better than others

4. I'm worse than others

5. I hate _____ (fill in the blank)

6. I'm not whole unless I have a partner

7. I don't need anybody

8. I need to be in control

9. I want power

10. I want people to do things for me

11. I wish that person was dead

12. I wish I had never been born

13. If I was rich or thin or good looking life would be a lot easier

14. I'd rather put effort into my looks than my education or career

15. I wish I could get even with everyone who has hurt me

16. If I handle people in certain ways (manipulation) I'll get what I want

17. I'll never be good enough so I'll just give up

18. Some things in life are too hard so why even try?

I'm sure you've had many of these thoughts throughout your life. You might have even had some of them within the last 24 hours, though perhaps you didn't notice. After some time, all of those negative thoughts become a constant hum in the background, though they're still doing damage and adding to your shadow.

One thing I want to say is that even if you don't fully believe any of those thoughts or would never act upon any impulses, simply thinking it still does harm. It becomes part of your shadow because you believe thinking such things is wrong when in reality a thought is just a thought, it's our attachment to it that creates problems.

For example, if I thought to myself right now, "I'm a seven-foot-tall discus thrower and was in the 1940 Olympics." That sounds silly, doesn't it? And in no way is it true, obviously. I know it's just a thought and let it go. Yet we cling to thoughts of being ugly, not good enough, too fat, not smart enough, our jealousy and anger, and so on. Thoughts are not reality. How much easier would life be and how much happier would you be if you finally made peace with your shadow?

Intimacy Blocks

Does the thought of loving someone deeply and being loved just as much in return scare you? If not, you're either one of the very few who has worked through every one of your shadows and has already found true love, found the right partner who will help you be your best and vice versa, or you're lying to yourself. Or, you've been single for a while and have forgotten about all of your baggage that rises to the surface when you're in a relationship.

Of course, we all want to love and be loved, it's natural, but intimate relationships also dredge up all of those uncomfortable feelings we hate facing. We might feel insecure or unworthy, and we soon find ourselves judging our partner more and more harshly as a way to protect ourselves. Tearing down your walls, daring to be your authentic self, and allowing someone to love you exactly as you are is scary.

Love is very much like a bottle of shaken champagne, along with all of the good feelings that burst to the surface will come everything else that needs to be cleared out as well. It's a lot to handle so the ego will jump in and do all it can to destroy any potential the relationship might have of surviving and thriving.

Remember, just as they're a mirror for you, you're a mirror for them. You both have something to learn from each other. So does that mean no matter how miserable you are or no matter how dysfunctional a relationship is you should stick it out? Not at all. I fully believe, have experienced, and have seen in others that shadow work in a relationship needs to be mutual or it won't work. Yes, you can work on yourself, but you can't force your partner to work on themselves or even work with you.

The key is, when you get into a new relationship, or even if you've been in one for a while, be observant of your actions and reactions, and always have compassion for yourself and your partner. Take notice of what bubbles up to the surface for you. Don't shut it out, judge it, or criticize it. Instead, do your work to name this shadow, own it, embrace it, and let it go.

Why We Reject Our Shadow

As spiritual beings, we know that our shadow is a natural part of us and isn't negative in the least. As human beings, we operate on survival mode though, even if we think we aren't. We will do anything to stay alive, stay away from danger, and save our mortal lives. Pain of any kind, but especially emotional pain, is perceived by our mind as a threat and we'll do all we can to protect ourselves.

As you can imagine, this backfires though because when we look inside ourselves we see all of that pain and try to run away from it, but you can't run away from yourself. All you can do is ignore it...again. Each time you encounter that type of pain it gets piled on to what you're already clinging to. Is it any wonder that the shadow self is so big and "scary"?

Another reason we reject our shadow traits is because society teaches us that these parts of ourselves aren't normal. If you show that you're angry, jealous, weak, sad, or afraid then you could be rejected. Our survival mode tells us if we're rejected we won't survive. Belonging to our tribe of humanity is important. Without others accepting us we feel isolated and vulnerable. So we learn, from a young age, to hide those parts of ourselves that others will find objectionable.

Rejecting your shadow comes with its own pain though because you're denying half of who you are. You're showing others only a portion of yourself, a one-sided person who possesses everything good and light. Living this way is not only tiring but unrealistic and something you won't be able to sustain for an entire lifetime. At some point, your shadow will make itself known. The more you ignore it, the bigger it becomes until you finally face it.

If It's So Hard, Why Do It?

Maybe you've already done some shadow work or are just now starting the journey. After reading why your shadow was created and everything that's stored in it, you might wonder why you should do shadow work at all. It's a dark journey filled with pain, discomfort, embarrassment, and the work itself feels like punishment. So why do it? Why put yourself through all of that when you've done such a great job of ignoring and dodging your shadow all these years?

Because, delving into those darkest parts of yourself will pay off big-time. You'll feel a sense of freedom, peace, compassion, and joy on a level that's beyond anything you've imagined. If you've already been doing shadow work and haven't discovered those feelings yet it's because you aren't finished. And this is where people give up.

Shadow work is like going through a hoarded house, piece by piece. You want your home clean and sparkling right away, but it took years to accumulate all of this stuff. Be gentle with yourself yet diligent and determined with your healing. If you do this, your life will be transformed.

While shadow work is actually pretty simple, by no means is it easy. If you aren't feeling emotional, angry, afraid, or nearly brought to your knees then you know you've only touched upon the work you need to do.

I had a client with a lot of emotional hangups and obstacles (as many of us have) who went through the shadow work exercises and told me it was a piece of cake and she was now a whole person. Healed forever. After having done my own shadow work for years now and helping clients on their paths, I knew this wasn't the case. I let her discover this on her own though since it's easier to learn something when you've experienced it yourself.

Sure enough, not soon after telling me this, she was faced with a recurring problem she had completely believed she'd healed from and left behind. The fact that it popped up again and she wasn't expecting it affected her more deeply than it ever had before.

Of course, I'm not the type to say, "I told you so". Instead, I helped her work through the issue and recommended she keep doing shadow work. I also let her know that once she had truly worked through the issue(s) she would know it.

She put it off for about six months because she wasn't ready, and that's okay! Not everyone is prepared to do such deep, emotional work right away. Some never are. We're all on our own paths in life, and everyone is at different stages. Even when you're working hard to make peace with your shadow side you'll have breakthroughs and setbacks. It's all part of the healing process.

Benefits Of Facing Your Shadow

We've talked a lot about all the negative aspects of hiding from your shadow and all the things we say and do that add to it over time. Now let's look at some benefits and rewards you'll experience once you integrate and accept your shadow.

1. Better Relationships

First and foremost, you'll notice that all your relationships become happier and more meaningful. Think of who you butt heads with, who makes you feel small, weak, or angry. This person is in your life, bringing your deepest wounds to the surface, so you can face them.

Soon, you'll no longer need to learn these "lessons" and you'll start attracting positive people into your life while those who aren't growing and changing will naturally drift away. And, once we know ourselves better and accept all parts within us, it's so much easier to accept others as well.

2. Higher Energy Levels

The bigger your shadow is the more exhausted you'll feel. If you're chronically low on energy then I can guarantee you have a lot of shadow work to do. Carrying around all of that self-imposed rejection is a heavy load. It takes a lot of energy to keep dragging it along with you day after day. Imagine how much freer you'll feel and how much better you'll feel once you dump that baggage and realize that your shadow isn't the bad guy after all.

Once you start admitting to and owning those shadow thoughts that have suffocated you for so long you'll be surprised at the energy coursing through you. I've felt it as a rush of warmth, a tingling sensation, or incredible surges. Other times it feels more like a weight being lifted, a lightness of being I hadn't known for some time.

The longer you've held on to a part of your shadow the more work it will take to release it, but the effort is worth it. Once the block is removed and your energy starts flowing again you'll wonder why you didn't do it sooner.

3. Greater Understanding

When you finally learn to accept yourself as you are—a whole person rather than a light side you show to the public and dark side you keep hidden—it will be easier for you to accept others. You'll have more compassion, love, and understanding for yourself and everyone you come in contact with. You'll see the best in others rather than passing judgment and you'll know that we're all doing our best with what we've got at the moment.

Having patience with life's processes will be easier as well. Whether you're standing in line at the grocery, working on your healing, or allowing relationships and situations to unfold as they should rather than trying to force them into what you're preconceived notions are.

Finding Better Mirrors

Remember how we were talking about the fact that everyone in your life is a mirror of who you are inside? The more seemingly negative a person is, the worse our personal relationships are, shows what we need to work on. Most of the time we just think, "What's wrong with that person! They're terrible! They don't treat me the way I deserve to be! They have horrible habits!" and so on. Since they *are* a mirror of yourself in some aspects though, it's incredibly helpful in showing where to roll up your sleeves and start working.

That doesn't mean you should surround yourself with people who constantly force you to face your shadow traits. Yes, work on them, you should! But over time start surrounding yourself with better mirrors. You want people who lift you up, who reflect your positive qualities, but also make you aware of the things you ignore or deny. It's far easier to see in others what we can't see in ourselves—the good and not so good.

So what does a good mirror look like in a person? They're emotionally stable, kind, and loving. They speak from the heart rather than the ego, and they never judge, ridicule, or shame others. You need people in your life who want to see you succeed and be happy. Even having just one person like this in your life is amazingly helpful. Treasure this relationship. In turn, try to be a good mirror for others as well.

If you don't have anyone in your life like this just yet, don't worry, you soon will. As you do more shadow work, more healing, and learning, you'll find that you outgrow some of your current relationships and they'll drift away. This is because they'll no longer be a mirror of some old part of you. On a subconscious level, you won't recognize or feel a connection to this person any longer and you'll attract other mirrors.

I've had countless clients tell me that as they progressed on their spiritual path they lost long-time friends and wondered if they did something wrong or why the friend changed so much. If you find yourself mourning over the loss of one or more friendships I'm letting you know that you didn't do anything wrong. It's the fact that you're changing, and that's a good thing.

Over time you'll attract people who are on your current energy level. People who are more positive mirrors. People who encourage you and help you to become your authentic self.

Making Time For Shadow Work

Although you don't have to go into this with an all-or-nothing mindset, you will need to make it a habit to work on your shadow. You'll also need to take breaks from it periodically. If you want to finally integrate with this part of yourself and ultimately live life as your authentic self it's going to take persistence and dedication.

You don't need to spend hours a day on it, nor do you need to do it every single day. Making it a routine though will be helpful. Some people set aside ten minutes a day, while others prefer to tackle shadow work on the weekends only but do it for a bit longer. I recommend no more than half an hour each time, though do what feels best for you.

A word of warning though is that doing it for too long can wear you out and create more problems than you're trying to overcome. I also suggest not doing any shadow work if you're ill, stressed, or didn't get enough sleep the night before. You want to be in a good mindset and have the energy to see the session through.

Something very different about shadow work compared to other spiritual paths is that it's solely for those who are seeking the truth. *Their* truth. It's all about confronting yourself and facing your darkness. Each time you do you might feel shaken up or exhausted, but soon after you'll enter a state of quiet calm and acceptance.

Although it sounds stressful, it's important to try to relax when doing these exercises. I always suggest starting shadow work with a few minutes of calming meditation or just relaxing and listening to nature sounds or gentle music. Sometimes I'll do a short and gentle yoga routine to relax me and get me into the right mindset.

As you're doing the exercises, avoid passing judgment on yourself or criticizing what you find. Trust me, it won't be flattering or pretty in there. Regardless of what comes up, remind yourself that it's just a thought and you don't need to react to it. The memory or feeling is simply trying to tell you something, to make you aware of the fragmented pieces living inside you. Just breathe through any rough feelings that surface and know that these thoughts and memories don't define you.

Show yourself compassion and understanding rather than feeling embarrassed, guilty, or angry. Condemning your feelings will undo all the shadow work you've done so far and make you feel awful.

While you're on the journey of shadow work it's good to keep a journal to write down or draw anything you discover. By keeping notes you'll be able to keep track of your progress and will find your healing journey far more effective. You'll probably also find connections that you hadn't realized before.

Shadow Work Changes Over Time

During your healing process the way you practice shadow work will change based on what you've already accomplished, your experiences, understanding, and beliefs. If you've already done some work, the next time you approach it will be different because you aren't the same person you were when you started this journey.

As you delve deeper, uncovering more layers of your darker side, there's often a tendency to run back to the light. We don't like the feelings we find there and immediately start judging ourselves. We believe we're being ridiculous for storing that old memory and the emotions that go along with it and wonder why we just can't get over it already.

One time I uncovered something that hurt me deeply as a child, though as an adult it seemed so small and insignificant. We were at my cousin's house playing outside and I saw my mom leaving with my sister in the car. I was terrified and went running to the car screaming for her to stop. She did so but told me to stay there and play with my cousin and they'd be right back. She said she was just getting dinner for everyone. In my mind, as a ten-year-old, I honestly believed she wasn't coming back. I cried, feeling abandoned until she returned.

Of course, other things in my life had happened before this incident to make me think I was being abandoned by my mother. At that point, I hadn't discovered where the initial shadow took hold though.

When that memory sprang up during a session of shadow work, my knee-jerk reaction had me turning away from it. I thought how incredibly dramatic I had been back then, and that I should just let it go since my mother obviously came back.

Those parts of us don't grow though. That memory-shard still felt exactly like an abandoned 10-year-old. So why was I being so harsh to my child-self? Why was I angry and disgusted with her when she was still so afraid and had every right to be?

So, I took another look at the memory, this time allowing it to unfold in all its emotional glory, so to speak. The fear felt overwhelming though I breathed through it. I admitted to myself that my mother had indeed abandoned me in several ways throughout my childhood. I didn't need to feel embarrassed or ashamed that I felt that way at that moment all those years ago.

Then a wonderful thing happened. When I offered the child part of me a chance to fully feel that fear and get it all out, when she finally had someone to listen to her, the memory seemed far less sharp and jagged. It didn't completely disappear, but it eased up and the edges were a lot smoother than they used to be.

We're human and we go through traumatic things in life. As we observe those around us and are immersed in one or another emotional event, we hold on to it or let it go, depending on what's already in our shadow.

Using my example above, as you can tell, one of the things I've always been afraid of is abandonment. Each time I experienced something that made me worry that I'd possibly be abandoned it became another layer in my shadow. Over time, it grew and grew. Just acknowledging my fear of abandonment wasn't enough to heal, I needed to peel back layer after layer and re-experience each episode.

Of course, some memories are so much a part of you and so long-forgotten that you won't be able to uncover all of them. That's okay though. As long as you're working with whatever you find, you'll eventually dissolve and integrate with those parts of your shadow.

When you're doing your own work, do your best not to judge, ridicule, or hide away from the darkness. If you can, observe these shadow memories and let them unfold. If you feel brave enough, immerse yourself in those old feelings and see what they have to say and what they can teach you.

These emotions you find in those dark places are raw and honest. It's how you truly felt and might still feel. This is why shadow work is so powerful and why it takes so long to work through it. Just when you thought you uncovered the reason for one of your shadows, you dig a little deeper and find something else.

Each time you encounter one of these fragments, your job is to:

- Identify it.

What's the event and the emotion attached to it? So many of our shadows have been hidden in the unconscious part of the mind. They will always come to the surface though and you'll notice them because something will trigger you. You'll feel anger, fear, sadness, disgust, or another emotion that has you yet again rejecting this part of yourself.

- Accept it.

Yes, the event happened, but it's in the past and you don't have to let it control you. By accepting your shadows and owning them you acknowledge that they had a purpose in protecting you somehow. Although they feel negative, every piece of your shadow has value.

- Love it.

Rather than denying or judging, send love and understanding to this dark feeling. When you offer compassion rather than condemnation you allow your shadows to come into the light. By doing this, they become part of you rather than those areas of your personality you continue to hide from.

- Integrate it.

Know that your emotions are valid and that it's okay to feel this way. Every part of your shadow has value, and by embracing them you allow them to evolve and eventually help you rather than hinder you.

- Keep at it.

Shadow work is a lifelong process, though gets easier over time. This is not a one-and-done type of session. If you went to see a therapist would you be whole and healed after one visit? No.

Sometimes you'll learn something new when you do an exercise. Other times you'll reprocess something you thought you'd already let go of. If an issue pops up again know that you need to discover more about this particular shadow and just go with it rather than rolling your eyes and thinking, "This again?" You'll know when a certain part has been healed because it won't have the same hold over you as it did before.

Getting to Work

Although you don't need to do anything formal to do shadow work—you can simply go somewhere quiet and dive right in—I've found it extremely helpful to do a little prepping beforehand. Doing so sends the message to your mind that what you're about to embark on is important and special, allowing your session to go more smoothly and be more helpful.

Then again, there will be times when a shadow will pop up seemingly out of nowhere. If you can, stop for a moment and see what it's trying to share with you. This happened to me once when I was at work getting a granola bar from the vending machine.

It was the last one and it got stuck. I became frustrated as I repeatedly pushed the button and banged on the machine, hoping to dislodge my snack. I then noticed a shadow surfacing as my irritation grew larger than the situation called for. I knew this part of myself was trying to share something with me so I sat at a nearby table for a moment, took a few cleansing breaths, and let it run its course.

As I sat there, a memory surfaced of when I was a child, probably around seven. I was at home getting a snack. It was the last granola bar in the box and I was really looking forward to it. My stepfather then walked into the kitchen and snatched it from my hand saying, "This is mine!" Food scarcity was all too common in my life from birth until I moved out at the age of 16. I remember always feeling hungry when I lived with my parents.

I hadn't thought about the granola bar incident with my step-father once until that moment at the vending machine. My out-of-the-ordinary frustration over a simple snack could be traced back to hunger as a child. I let the memory play out, allowed it to pour through me and show me its pain, and then it faded.

Normally, I wouldn't want to do any type of shadow work in public, especially not at work, but I recognized it as important and knew that if I waited to do it when I got home my feelings would have eased up and I might not have been able to recapture the intensity of that memory.

Most of the time you'll want to work on your healing journey while at home or some other quiet place where you feel safe and won't be disturbed. Now, let's roll up our sleeves and get to work! I'll have more exercises later on but let's start here.

1. Create A Special Environment

The process of dredging up your shadows will be challenging, to say the least. By creating a comfortable and special environment you're letting your conscious and subconscious know that what you're about to do is important but that you're in a safe place to do so.

I almost always do my sessions in my bedroom. I light incense, a few candles, play soothing nature sounds, and have a mug of chamomile tea ready. And, of course, I have my journal and pen. There's something so personal and cathartic about writing something down by hand.

2. Think and Feel

You don't need to meditate or spend a long time on this. Just sit with your eyes closed and breathe normally. Now think about some of the things you don't like about yourself. What are the parts of you that you reject, despise, or keep hidden? You could mentally name each thing then choose to focus on just one for now and allow yourself to feel everything that comes along with this thought.

One (of the several) things I haven't liked about myself is that I've always been overweight. I've been on diets, exercised like mad, and have lost weight in the past only to put it back on. I don't eat horribly and I go for walks several times a week, hike with my family, garden, and do other physical activities. But, between a thyroid problem, menopause, "fat-genes", and a huge shadow that's filled with too many years of not having enough food, it's like a losing battle.

While it's true that I could probably keep doing shadow work on this issue and perhaps one day overcome it, I've learned to be more accepting and find balance. I try to be as healthy as I can, but also not a diet or exercise fanatic.

3. Notice Your Reactions

As these feelings and any memories start surfacing pay attention to your emotions. Is there shame? Anger? Sadness? Fear? Or something else?

How does your body feel? You might experience chills, pain, shaking, sweating, tightness in your chest or throat, breathing heavier, or unconsciously tensing your fists. Whenever I hit upon something important I notice that I clench my teeth.

Your first instinct will probably be to end these uncomfortable feelings but do your best to relax and stay with all of it. Remind yourself that all of this is perfectly natural and shows that you're processing the shadow at long last.

4. Name Your Shadow

When this shadow surfaces label it. It might be "Money", "Food", "Love", "Neglect", "Abandonment", or anything you associate with this darker part of you.

Also, pay attention to any people that come to mind. This could be a person who taught you to feel this way, such as my stepfather making me feel angry for taking away my food. It could also be a person you don't like because they're a mirror of that shadow part of you.

At my last job, there was a woman who weighed well over 400 pounds. She was nice enough, but I just didn't like her for some reason. When I did some shadow work related to my childhood hunger she popped into my mind.

I asked myself why she would be part of this shadow and I realized it was a mirror into myself. Some part of me didn't like her because she obviously ate far too much food and my child self was upset that I had never had enough to eat. The little girl inside me felt it wasn't fair and she let me know!

What about my adult self though? I was honest and recognized that because I'm overweight I was afraid of getting bigger and bigger. That didn't happen, I've been at the same weight for decades now, but it worried me nonetheless.

When I discovered this I wrote down the name of this shadow part of myself in my journal. I labeled it "hunger" and listed all the people that played a part—either knowingly or unknowingly—in adding to it over the years.

Can you see how many facets just one part of your shadow holds? That's why this is such a long journey, though the rewards are endless.

5. Stream-Of-Consciousness Writing

Once you've delved into one or more of your shadows, felt them, and named them, you can continue on and do stream-of-consciousness writing in your journal. As you focus on the current shadow at hand, put your pen to the paper and get it all out. Just write, write, write, and don't stop until you feel there's nothing more left inside you at the moment. Don't censor yourself. Don't judge yourself. Don't try to write perfectly or politely. Just... write...

At first, you might get stuck or have no idea where to begin, but as you keep going you'll notice that you eventually reach the depths of your emotions as your subconscious takes over and does all the writing.

Sometimes I'll get whole paragraphs, while other times I'll write short sentences or simply lists of words. Other times it's as if the child part of me is speaking while at others it's almost like my higher self or a guide has come through. Continue writing for as long as you'd like. Very often I've done only a couple of minutes and during a few sessions, I've written for an hour or longer.

When you're finished and you look over everything you've put down in your journal you'll probably be surprised by what came out. Some stuff will be old news that you've gone over dozens or even thousands of times in your mind before. Other things might be brand new.

One time when I was doing this exercise something completely out of the blue came to the surface. I was writing about things that made me feel shame. Everything I wrote down was things I'd covered before, but I was okay with it since rehashing things is how we eventually overcome them.

In the next moment I wrote down the sentence, "I hate pink carpet!" This was accompanied by feelings of extreme embarrassment. I instantly felt sweat popping out on my upper lip and hairline. I knew this was important!

I asked myself why I hate pink carpeting and allowed whatever it was to take center stage. I then recalled an incident from when I was about six years old. I was with a friend visiting her grandmother. I had to go to the bathroom so badly but felt uncomfortable in this woman's home. Finally, I asked to use the restroom, rushed to it, but didn't make it to the toilet in time. I stood there on the pink carpet and wet my pants. I felt so embarrassed!

When it happened, criticism started flooding my young mind. "Only babies pee themselves! You're a big girl, why did you do this? You're disgusting and dirty now! Nobody will like you because you're a baby who wets her pants!" In reality, nobody was angry with me and they helped me, but that moment of intense shame had already taken up residence in my shadow at some point in the past and this incident only added to it.

As all of this came out I was not only surprised, but I felt so much compassion toward my child self. I mentally hugged her and even laughed, gently, at feeling so embarrassed over something that was merely an accident. To this day, I still don't like pink carpeting, but when I see it now I smile rather than feel a wave of self-disgust and shame.

6. Asking Questions

If you get stuck or find that you can't dig any deeper into your subconscious, you can write: Who? What? When? Where? Why? Choose one of these and see what you can bring to the surface.

For example, let's say you're working on finances. You want to get to the root cause of your money problems but nothing's coming up. You could write down, "Why am I bad with my money?" Or, "Who taught me these negative money lessons?" Or, "Where do I struggle most with money?" Or, "When did my financial problems first take hold?"

Of course, you'll want to write your question down in a way that would prove helpful to you, and you might not hit pay-dirt right away, so keep digging. You'll know you struck gold when you feel that sensation of "Ah-ha! This is it!" It might not be the only "it" but is the one you're supposed to cover during this session.

I sometimes like writing things down as conversations between one part of myself and another part. I did one on money before and it went something like this:

"How do you feel about money?"

"Bad."

"Why?"

"I hate it."

"Why?"

"I need it but don't like having it."

"Why?"

"Because you have to work so hard but it's gone so fast."

"Why else?"

"Because my parents often argued about money when I was a kid."

"How did that make you feel?"

"Scared."

"Why?"

"Because they would start yelling and get really loud and it would scare me."

"Why did it scare you?"

"Because I thought they would do something to hurt each other or me."

It was then that I realized how deep my financial subconscious programming went. Not only did I grow up with parents who spent money on drugs and booze rather than rent and food, so my mind already believed money was scarce, but there was fear of abuse behind money as well. No wonder I got rid of every last penny as soon as it came in!

Remind yourself too that just because you find out where a shadow came from doesn't mean it vanishes. As aggravating as it may seem, it's fully entrenched and is part of you. That's why it's best to make friends with your shadows and learn to work with them and get them to work with you rather than against you.

Finding The Positive In Your Shadows

I'm sure it seems by now that all of those traumas and experiences that eventually became part of your shadow self seem horrible and in no way beneficial. That's simply not true though. The messages you receive from these seemingly hidden parts of yourself are trying to tell you something and teach you something. Your shadow wants to help you heal.

So how do we find out how our shadow is trying to help us?

1. Make a list of every negative shadow trait that comes to mind right now. Don't think too hard about it and don't try to cover a lot of territory at the moment. You'll have plenty of time to work on more issues later.

When I did this exercise I wrote down:

- I'm fat

- I'm stupid

- I'll never be successful

- Something bad always happens

- I feel scared

- I'll always be a broken person

Wow, that seems pretty harsh, doesn't it? Would you say any of this to someone you cared about? Of course not. And yet we subconsciously repeat so many negative comments to ourselves daily. We also allow it to color our world and dictate our actions. But what if we stopped for a moment and looked at each one of those so-called negative qualities, turned them around, and tried to see the positive aspects of them?

Choose each of your "flaws" and write down how it can help teach you something about yourself and how you can grow and heal. When I did this it was difficult trying to find anything positive in all of that garbage. It just felt bad and I didn't want to think about any of it. I knew the exercise was important for my soul growth though so I stepped outside of myself and pretended I was giving a friend advice. I'll choose a few from my above list and show you how I did it.

"I'll always be a broken person."

Everything you've been through has helped you to be stronger. You've overcome so much! You just need to reprogram your way of thinking and see that everything you consider as a weakness in you is truly a strength that has helped you to survive and thrive.

"I feel scared."

This isn't a bad thing. It shows that you're in touch with your emotions and you're allowing your shadows to surface so you can process them. It's showing you what's important and what you need to work on.

"I'm stupid."

No, you aren't. That's just what your stepfather wanted you to believe. You're smart and learning more every day.

"I'm fat."

Your weight has been a mental and emotional cushion against the things and people in this world that have hurt you or that you worried would hurt you. As an adult, you have a choice to eat better and exercise. It's not easy, but slow and steady wins the race.

"Something bad always happens."

A lot of good things happen too, but believing something bad will eventually happen shows that you should use that worry to prepare yourself "just in case". If you're prepared then you'll feel more confident and eventually you won't always believe something bad will happen. Most things we view as bad are either out of our control or something we could have planned better for but didn't.

As you can see, I gave myself a little pep-talk and showed myself how I could take those shadow traits and learn something from them. Nothing is all bad or all good. The best thing you can do for yourself is to face your shadows and take a good look at how they can help you, how they have helped you, and how you can grow from them and learn to work with them. Consider your shadows the fuel you need to improve yourself and your life.

Owning Your Shadow

No matter how long you've been doing shadow work, or how much you think you've finally made it to the end of the journey, there will always be more layers revealed to you. You will always experience breakthroughs, large and small, until you leave this current life.

In the beginning, you can get a whole lot of shadow work done in a relatively short amount of time. As the years pass, you'll find that new discoveries come through, though not as consistently as when you first started this work. Know that when the time is right, when you're meant to address this certain shadow aspect of yourself, it will make itself known.

But how do you know if a thought or feeling is truly a shadow trait that needs to be worked on? How can you face it and eventually own these parts of yourself? The most revealing question you can ask yourself is, "Where do I judge others?"

The shadows we ignore or deny most are what we judge in others. These are the parts of us that we feel no connection to but are truly the biggest parts of the shadow self. If you aren't facing some aspect of yourself you're going to project it outward onto others. You do this completely subconsciously, but what you see most often in others that you dislike is a loud and clear message that this is where work needs to be done.

Here are a couple of personal examples:

- I detest taking naps. In the past, when I found out someone regularly liked to nap I automatically labeled them as lazy, which made me dislike them. Doesn't that seem ridiculous? For too many years I never questioned why I felt this way. I assumed it was because I was always "busy" and didn't have the luxury of taking naps since I worked, had five kids, and a heaping plate of other responsibilities. No matter how tired I was or how sick I felt I refused to take a nap.

One day I admitted to myself that the reason I have such a bad view of napping is because my mother pretty much slept throughout my childhood due to drug use. She rarely worked, never cleaned the house, and neglected my sister and me. Okay, so I knew where this shadow came from, but that didn't mean I resolved it.

It took a long time, but whenever I felt my inner critic rise to the surface regarding napping, I reminded myself that it had nothing to do with the person being lazy, but was simply a part of my past that needed healing.

- Another shadow I struggled with was regarding intelligence. I either labeled people as smart or dumb. When I dated I always gravitated toward men who had at least a Master's Degree and who I deemed to be very intelligent. Simply put, brains turned me on.

What I didn't take into account is, regardless of a person's education or background, it doesn't really make them "smart". They could use big words and talk about their brainy careers all they wanted to, but I discovered that, like all people, they had strengths and weaknesses. Having a high IQ didn't make them kinder than others. Also, most had no sense of humor, lacked commonsense, and had poor communication skills. (Not all, but several I had dated.)

I already knew where this shadow came from though. It was because my stepfather often ridiculed me and called me stupid. He would take every opportunity to show me how "dumb" I was. So, I did everything in my power to prove him wrong and excelled when I was in school for medical assisting and medical office management. I had a 4.0 GPA, was on the honor roll, but that didn't take care of that shadow though. If nothing, it made it worse because I now felt better than him.

I could now see how unintelligent he truly was and that he tormented me for so many years just because he was a bully, not because I was dumb. While this was all true, it made me dislike "stupid" people even more since they reminded me of my stepfather. As you can imagine, this shadow was huge since I now had two reasons to dislike people who I deemed had low intelligence.

As I got older and started doing shadow work I realized that this was just me projecting onto others. Once I learned to work through this dark side of myself I realized how unfair it was of me to judge others based on my own emotions and experiences. Also, not having to prove how smart I was all the time was a huge weight off my shoulders. It was okay to not know everything. I didn't need to be a walking encyclopedia to be loved and accepted.

Pay attention to where you judge others. The harsher your inner criticism the bigger the shadow inside you. Notice what triggers your anger. If you despise something in others or if something ticks you off it's because you're ignoring the thing in your shadow that's trying to teach you something. Anything that gets our attention, typically in a bad way, is an opportunity to learn something about ourselves and eventually make peace with it.

Loving Your Shadows

If anything is an advanced shadow exercise, this is it. It's so hard for us to learn to even accept our shortcomings and supposed flaws, let alone love them. We've spent a lifetime believing that these traits are better left ignored or, when they do surface, to battle against.

You wouldn't ridicule a baby for not being able to walk or talk, and you wouldn't turn your back on a friend who's in pain or lecture them about being so "weak". No, you would empathize with them and have compassion. Extend this same level of care and understanding to your shadow self that's in the process of healing. View your shadow traits with loving eyes and bring this same love to all those stuck, dark areas inside and accept where you are in the journey.

One thing to keep in mind is that even though you're sending love and acceptance to your shadow doesn't mean you're healed and have made peace with everything. Instead, think of it as if you had an argument with a friend or relative. You care about them, but you might not get over that episode right away. Even so, you still send them love and know that your anger will eventually dissolve.

As you go about your days, if any of your shadow fragments pop up, accept it and send love to it. Remind yourself that you are *not* your shadows. Know that its purpose is to get your attention so that you can continually better yourself. It came up for a reason. Something triggered it and wants you to acknowledge it.

Once you learn to love all of yourself, every part, you'll experience power and freedom that you might never have known before. You'll find that you feel far more genuine, compassionate, and courageous for having learned how to embrace those "ugly" parts of yourself. You'll also be far more accepting of other people's less desirable traits because you can see the lesson and potential for growth hidden beneath it all.

Does that mean that once you fully accept yourself that all others will accept and appreciate you for being authentic and honest? No. We're all on different learning paths in life and we need to release that survival mindset of needing to be accepted. As long as you're living your own truth, it doesn't matter what others think about you.

I used to be a people-pleaser to the max. I wanted—no, I _needed_—everyone to like me. If they didn't I felt hurt, torn, sad, depressed, and angry. After all, if someone didn't like all these good parts I was careful to only show, what would they think if they saw all those bad parts? It was terrifying for me to even imagine.

So I tried harder to be everything to everyone. I overextended myself, I bit my tongue, I was agreeable and helpful, and was certain to always wear a bright smile—no matter how sad or tired or angry I felt inside.

Not until I started doing my own shadow work and realizing that people who truly loved me, would love me unconditionally, was I able to be my authentic self. I could finally work on those razor-sharp pieces inside of me and not be afraid.

Sure, I lost some friends along the way. People who wondered why I had changed so much, why I wasn't as helpful or available any day, any time. I lost a job because I no longer volunteered to work overtime, weekends, and come in on days off to fill in for someone who was on vacation. (Meanwhile, I hadn't taken a vacation in the entire five years I'd worked there.) And, yes, even my kids wondered "what was up with Mom" when I no longer stayed up all night sewing a Halloween costume at the last minute or because I cried, or got angry, or voiced an honest opinion that they weren't happy with.

Those who truly care about me stuck my side and have admired me for my growth, loving that I'm a real person now and no longer wear a mask of what I thought they wanted to see. When I realized I was still lovable and accepted (warts and all!) I breathed a sigh of relief and have never gone back to the one-dimensional person I used to be. I've allowed myself to be myself.

Rather than continuing to stuff my shadow down I took it by the hand and brought it along with me wherever I went. I finally let it step out into the light. Was it a smooth transition? Not at all. There were times when my shadow took over and I acted in ways that, before, would have shocked or embarrassed me.

Now I know that those incidences were just darker sides of my personality running wild because I'd stifled them for too long. After a while, through love and acceptance, they calmed down and actually became helpful to my life. Now I set boundaries rather than saying yes to everyone and letting others use and abuse me. I confidently speak from my heart rather than from fear of being rejected or ridiculed.

Though the journey was sometimes difficult, I have nothing but gratitude for my shadow since it showed me how to evolve into the whole person I am today. Is the journey over? Am I completely healed? Has every shadow been integrated and embraced? Not at all. It's a continuous process of always evolving, though now I see it as a gift, as an opportunity to learn and grow rather than something to be ashamed of and hide from the world.

Digging Deeper

Maybe you already know some of the shadows lurking inside you, but very often we're blind to most of them or have only scratched the surface of the ones we're aware of. Stream-of-consciousness writing is an excellent way to uncover or even rediscover places where you need to heal or improve.

I talked about stream-of-consciousness writing a bit ago and I cover it in many of my books because it's so helpful in getting to the root of things and freeing those stuck places inside. Also called free-writing, word painting, chain of thought writing, among other things, all you need is a pen and a journal or pad of paper. I prefer this to typing on the computer since there's something very personal about seeing your thoughts in your own writing.

All you need to do is write three pages of notes each day for at least a week and see what starts showing up. Don't think about what you're writing, just let it all fall out.

I've found that the best time to do this exercise is in the morning when I first wake up or before going to bed. Yes, most of what you get will likely be worries, anxieties, random thoughts, and the like, but you'll also uncover some things that will get your attention. Those things that are dredged up from the subconscious and brought out into the open for you to take a good look at and learn more about. Things you need to heal from, learn from, or let go of.

You'll find things you never knew were there or that you didn't know were "that bad". You might find that you're still angry, hurt, or confused over an incident that happened months or even decades ago. You could find that you've been more stressed than you thought you were about something and any number of other truths that spill out.

One time when I did this exercise I discovered how unhappy I was at this one job I had at the time. It paid well, the people were nice, but it was a lot of responsibility and not something I truly wanted for myself at the time. Everyone thought I should be happy, even grateful, to have this position, but through this exercise it allowed me to be honest with myself.

How did that job tie in with my shadow though? For so long I felt I needed a high-paying job with a fancy title so people would look up to me—accept me, like me, love me. It made me feel smart and successful, but it also left me feeling overworked and exhausted. I had enough responsibilities at home and didn't want more piled on me. This job started affecting quality time with my family, but I was in denial...until I did this exercise.

When I saw my true thoughts and feelings on paper I couldn't ignore them any longer. I started looking for a slower-paced job with better hours so I could spend more time with my kids. Not even a week later I found one and never looked back. I was happier and felt like an enormous burden was lifted from my shoulders and my shadow felt lighter.

Something else I uncovered when doing this exercise another time was how unhappy I was in a (then) current relationship. On paper, we were the perfect couple, but in reality, I struggled to feel the attraction. He seemed to be everything I'd want in a guy. He was super intelligent, had a great job, his own home, he was funny, attractive, he liked my family, they liked him...but I felt zero chemistry.

Also, my intuition kept telling me that he was keeping something hidden, but I couldn't put my finger on it. I second-guessed myself and assumed it was because I had been in my fair share of dysfunctional relationships so I automatically believed this man was hiding something from me.

For three months I tried to make it work and if I hadn't done this exercise I might have stayed in the relationship longer. After all, I'd stayed in far worse relationships for much, much longer.

One night I started writing in my journal, dumping everything my brain felt compelled to, when I landed on this entry, "This isn't going to work, no matter how hard I try. I'm just not feeling it." After I wrote that I stopped for a moment, my heart beating faster, as guilt swam to the surface. I knew exactly what this pertained to, even if I didn't want to admit it out loud just yet.

After a few shaky breaths I closed my eyes and admitted to myself that the only reason I had kept trying to make things work with this man was because he was 100% invested in the relationship and had even started making future plans. Everything seemed exactly as I'd wanted it, but I couldn't deny my true feelings any longer.

I called him and told him how I felt, that I thought he was awesome but it just wasn't working for me. I said that I needed time to be single and work on some personal things, which was true.

Well...I discovered at that moment what he kept hidden: a horrible temper. He screamed and ranted and said some very demeaning things. I hung up and thanked that shadow for coming to the surface and getting my attention! Afterward, he texted me and emailed me with awful messages, showing that he, too, needed to work on his own shadows. I didn't reply to any of them since I had already said my peace.

Will you find something valuable or eye-opening every single time you do this exercise? With confidence, I say yes. Even if you already know the stuff that comes out, even if it seems to only pertain to your everyday life and nothing deeper, or if the words don't resonate with you at all, I guarantee there's something useful there.

As to how long you should continue to do this exercise, I'll leave that up to you. When I first started I did stream-of-consciousness writing every day for three solid months. I uncovered a lot, much of which was painful though necessary to purge. After those few months though I didn't feel the need to keep doing it daily.

Now, I only do this exercise when I feel that something is brewing beneath the surface and I know I need to find out what it is. Or, I might need to vent, worry, or wonder, in my journal and very often I see how it relates to an old shadow that I thought I took care of long ago.

Again, your shadow will always be part of you. You can't erase it. The key is, learning to work with your shadow and using its lessons to help you in life rather than holding you back.

Becoming More Aware

Another good way to become conscious of the parts of yourself that you're rejecting or hiding from is to use sentence prompts in your journal. Doing this helps to bring those things to the surface in a healthy and safe way. Rather than waiting for someone to trigger one of your shadow traits, you can work on them from the comfort of your own home while you're alone.

Where do you start though? What shadow themes do you need to work on most? What's hiding just out of view? Here's a list of journal prompts to choose from. You can start with the first one and go down the list over the coming days/weeks, or pick and choose which ones resonate with you most at this time.

Some of the following prompts will be more difficult than others to write about and be honest about. Even as I look over this list right now some of the questions make me feel uncomfortable, which tells me I still need to work on them.

Remind yourself that the more emotion something (or someone) triggers, or the more you want to avoid something (or someone), it's an indicator that this is a major part of your shadow. It's something that eventually needs to be faced, owned, integrated, and let go of.

1. In which ways do I feel powerless?

2. In which ways do I feel powerful?

3. How do I display my feelings of power or powerlessness?

4. How do I try to control situations or people?

5. How do I allow situations or people to control me?

6. Do I want to be sexually in control of my partner or my partner to be in control? Why?

7. Do I feel I deserve to be richer, happier, or better off than others? If so, why?

8. Do I feel less than others? Why?

9. In which ways do I envy other people? (Love, money, possessions, etc.)

10. In what ways do I feel damaged or unlovable?

11. In which way do people use me or I use others?

12. What do I hate in others, especially people in my family or social circle?

13. In which ways do I judge others?

14. What do I feel others are judging me about?

15. What things bother me the most about others or life in general?

16. When I think about the saddest part of my shadow, what comes to mind?

17. When I think about the angriest part of my shadow, what comes to mind?

18. Have I ever wished someone would die, or at least just disappear? Who and why?

19. Most recently, what situation or person has brought up intense feelings for me?

20. What situations make me feel the most uncomfortable? Why?

21. What are some of the benefits of doing shadow work?

22. How do I envision my life in the future, how will I be different, once I've done a good deal of shadow work?

When I first did this I went through the questions pretty quickly, doing all of them in just a couple of days. It seemed easy! But that told me I wasn't digging in deep enough. After that, I chose just one or two questions a day and wrote in my journal until nothing else would come out. Sometimes I got only a short paragraph, and at other times I got pages and pages. Sometimes I felt angry, embarrassed, shocked, or afraid. There were times I laughed, lovingly, at myself, and others when I cried and cried.

As you go over these prompts and answer them, you aren't necessarily trying to find anything new to uncover, though that just might happen. And you don't need to let your shadow completely take over either and fill the pages with nothing but emotional pain and anger. This is your safe space, your personal area to be free to vent and explore. Don't judge yourself and don't censor yourself.

Although each shadow fragment is a part of you, it doesn't limit you and it isn't the whole sum of who you are. The point of this exercise is to become aware, or more aware, of your darker traits and shine light on them so they're easier to work on. Once you're aware of them you then have a choice of how to handle it rather than being unconscious to these shadows and merely reacting to them.

Integrating The Shadow

I've mentioned a few times in this book about your shadows eventually dissolving, fading, or letting them go. This is more in a sense of acceptance rather than any shadow part of you actually vanishing. That's where shadow integration comes in.

A lot of people believe that if they work through their shadow traits they can eventually release them completely. They see it as working through karma, becoming enlightened, and ultimately living life as their higher selves without a trace of their former shadow. In reality, this isn't possible.

Your shadow is part of you, always will be, and should be. Everything exists in perfect balance in the universe, and you're no different. The key is, gaining balance over the light and dark parts of yourself, not trying to eradicate your shadow completely.

Humans have a way of ignoring or bypassing anything that brings up feelings of discomfort though. Rather than accepting those "less lovable" parts of ourselves and facing them with courage and honesty, we want to focus more on the light and on what's right in our lives. Ultimately, we hope that this part of ourselves becomes so much bigger and brighter that it shrinks our shadow down to nothing. This is simply living in denial.

As uncomfortable as it is, working with your shadow self actually creates balance and harmony. You become whole—mentally, emotionally, and spiritually. Denying your darker parts just creates a life of turmoil and conflict.

So what does it mean to integrate your shadow? When I talk about integrating your shadow I mean it in the sense of *owning* those parts so that you become whole. You're taking responsibility for your actions and your healing rather than rejecting or denying them. The rewards in doing this are a greater understanding of yourself and others, greater compassion, peace, and happiness.

In time, you'll find that you handle life so much better, especially when a shadow is triggered or you're faced with adversity. You'll function normally rather than lashing out, breaking down, falling apart, or closing yourself off. A fragmented person will almost always handle situations from various parts of their shadow because there's no wholeness in their center. This is why integration is so essential: it helps you to become whole again.

That all sounds great, right? So how do you go about integrating all those shadow parts of yourself?

1. Become more aware of the things about yourself that are difficult to admit to and face. For example, it was hard for me to admit that I was such a perfectionist that at times others saw me as very rigid. I prefer seeing myself as kind, loving, and flexible. But, I had to remind myself that although those are all true, the exact opposite lives inside me as well and sometimes surfaces.

2. When a shadow fragment rises up name it. For example, I might say something like this to myself, "I feel angry right now as I see this woman with a huge Coach purse. It reminds me of being poor as a child and I see purchases like this as something frivolous."

3. When you have time alone, recall this shadow trait and have a conversation with it. You can either speak out loud or write in your journal. What does it want to tell you? Why did it surface to begin with? What's the first time you remember this shadow? What lesson can it teach you about yourself? Why is it hard to face it or release it?

4. Sit with this shadow feeling for a moment and fully step into it. This is often difficult to do since our first instincts are to shove it away and get on to better feelings. If you feel angry, envious, sad, nervous, or any other so-called negative feeling, just let it wash over you.

Allow any thoughts, images, memories, or other feelings to fill you from head to toes. Again, this isn't easy to do, but just breathe through it and send this wounded part of yourself love and light.

You'll know that you're integrating with this shadow when that wave of intense emotion starts fading away. Our shadows are very much like a crying baby. The longer you ignore it the louder it cries. When you pay attention to it and offer love it will calm down.

5. Once the shadow emotion has receded congratulate yourself on sitting with this discomfort. All of these years you've either

ignored it or reacted to it. This time you actually worked with it and gave it a voice. Best of all, nothing bad happened while this shadow took over.

As time goes on and different aspects of your shadow surface here and there, you'll be able to handle these situations far better than you ever have before.

But what good is merging with all of this pain, anger, and heartache? Logically, it would seem like ridding yourself of these negative feelings would be optimal. But, you're a soul in a human body and you're always meant to grow and learn. As I've said before, everything needs to be in balance—both the good and the bad, the light and the darkness. From a spiritual perspective, it's how things are meant to be.

Your shadow offers valuable help and information, enabling you to reach ever-higher. If you think about it, totally ridding yourself of your entire shadow would mean you stop growing. Who wants that to happen? Not me. And I don't think you do either.

When some part of your darker side makes itself known it means there's a lesson to be learned or more healing to be done. I've had clients who thought they completely healed from something years ago, only to have a shadow trait pop up seemingly out of nowhere.

In my own experience, I remember thinking that I had worked through all of my shadows regarding finances. Life was good, I was making a lot of money, I felt happy, free, and on top of the world. And then a shadow jumped to the surface. My financial castle fell into rubble and I was back where I started. This was a very humbling experience, reminding me that my shadows are always there. Thinking that I totally eradicated them from my life was a huge mistake.

Instead, if I had known better back then, I would have realized that this financial shadow would always be part of me. I would have been more aware of when it was trying to get my attention and would have worked with it rather than ignoring it until it was screaming so loud the walls fell in on me.

Our shadows offer us enormous benefits if we learn to listen to them, accept them, and be aware of them rather than rejecting them. I've even learned to laugh with my shadow. Something will get my attention and create some intense emotion in me. I then smile and laugh, telling myself, "There's that money shadow again!" (Or whatever is trying to get my attention at the time.) Being aware is half the battle.

You can't eliminate your shadow and you really wouldn't want to. Without all of those "less acceptable" parts, you'd only be a shell of a person. It's not realistic to think we should walk around smiling all the time, no care in the world, with only love and joy flowing through our veins. As humans, we need each dark area for equilibrium. It makes us real and multi-faceted. Learn to see your shadow as a friend rather than an enemy.

Embracing The Shadow

Embracing our shadow selves doesn't mean we have the green light to act out on any emotion or desire that comes up. It's more about acknowledging and accepting that this shadow exists within you and then using it as an opportunity to learn more about yourself.

Indulging in your shadows and saying, "This is part of me. I accept it and will just go with it when it shows itself" will just backfire completely and make things worse. In fact, I had a friend who was like this. He was a spiritual person and very interested in doing shadow work, but he got it all wrong. Ever since I knew him he was afraid of showing any anger at all, even if the event called for it.

After doing some shadow work (not nearly enough!) he dove head-first into every dark aspect of his personality. Rather than acknowledging, owning, and integrating with his shadow, rather than seeing what lessons he could learn from it, he was like a match to gasoline. He would erupt in a fit of anger at the least provocation or anything that he felt seemed like a slight against him. He started becoming paranoid, suspicious, and a rage-a-holic.

As you can see, this is the exact opposite of who he used to be: mild-mannered, quiet, shy. He had become his shadow self day and night. Not until he had alienated every person who ever cared about him, lost his job, and his fiancee, did he wake up and realize he had been going about his healing path the wrong way. As the saying goes, "If you don't work it out you'll act it out".

Embracing your inner darkness means that you take responsibility for yourself, that you're aware of your shadow traits when they come up, but you don't need to act on them. Think of your shadows as private messages that are alerting you to something and for opportunities to grow. Acknowledge them rather than avoiding them and one day you'll find that they stop controlling you and can instead help you.

Exploring Your Shadow Through Art

There are many ways to explore your shadow and I covered some exercises in my first book *Shadow Work – Understanding and Making Peace With Your Darker Side*. It's important to not only acknowledge those hidden parts of you, but you need to face them and work on them as well.

It's not enough to merely say something like, "Yes, I know I have an anger problem" (or any other shadow you're dealing with) and never doing anything about it. That would be like knowing something is wrong with your car—you have a flat tire, you're almost out of gas, the engine is knocking—but you ignore it, thinking it will go away. It won't. Eventually, your car will break down and you'll be stranded.

The following exercises are some of my favorites for getting to the root of what's holding you back or holding you up. Those things in the subconscious that leap out when we least expect it, trying to get our attention, only to be banished to the darkness once again. You can try each of the following exercises, or choose the one(s) that calls to you right now then in the future give the others a try.

Any type of art, whether drawing, painting, or anything else along these lines is one of the highest forms of self-expression. When you put your pen, pencil, or paint to the paper you're allowing your shadow to have a voice, to come out and show itself.

In this exercise you'll go with the flow of your thoughts or emotions, creating whatever you're thinking or feeling. Don't worry about what comes out, don't focus on a theme if it doesn't come to you right away, just grab your pad of paper and tool of choice then let it all out.

There have been times when I've done art therapy and just drew many colored squiggles with crayons. Other times I've used paint and created colorful landscapes or dark forests. I've also used colored pencils, markers, and pastels. I have all of my art supplies in one plastic container so I can easily grab whatever I need when the mood strikes. You don't need to have a single artistic bone in your body to do this exercise either, I surely don't, but there's something incredibly freeing about expressing yourself through art.

I'll never forget this one session where I didn't have anything in mind but wanted to do some shadow work. At first, I colored some geometric shapes in different colors. I then felt an enormous burst of anger rising up in me and I grabbed a black crayon scribbling over the entire page! I felt my face getting hot and tears came to my eyes. Soon I was sobbing. Wow! Where did that come from?

After the wave of intensity faded I sat with my emotions, trying to catch my breath. I felt like I had just run a marathon! At first, no thoughts came to me, just raw anger. I took a few cleansing breaths and gave myself permission to feel whatever I needed to and to allow whatever was just below the surface to share its story with me.

A lot of childhood garbage came up, along with things from my two marriages as well. As I looked at my drawing I tried to see what it was telling me. For me, the colorful, geometric shapes represented times when life was going well and all the pieces fit together nicely and neatly.

Then there would always be some huge disruption—my mom taking a drug overdose and being in the hospital, my step-father having one-too-many drinks and going on a tirade, having to move once again because my parents got evicted, one of my husbands losing yet another job, an overdue bill coming in because we were now (again) a one-income household.

I could go on, but those are just some of the instances in my past that show how those nice, neat geometric patterns got scribbled over with chaos and uncertainty, which ultimately built up inside of me as anger. I _hated_ the instability and uncertainty during those times.

These memories were nothing new. They would bob to the surface here and there throughout my life, reminding me of where I came from and how I felt about it. I knew that angry, fearful child still lived inside me, as did the overwhelmed young mother. But as I looked more closely at my drawing I saw that, although there was angry scribbling over the top, a lot of the beautiful color still showed through. So what did this mean for me?

Yes, I had anger inside of me, and that's okay! I had every right to feel that way with the people dictating my life at the time—whether parents or partners. But I needed to remind myself that life isn't either/or. There will always be good times and hard times.

Now that I'm leading my own life without dysfunctional parents or partners, I can see that just because there were a lot of disruptions in my younger years that didn't mean life was all terrible all the time. There were still positive things I could look back on and hold close to me. I couldn't, and shouldn't, label my entire childhood or marriages as completely awful. Do I want to repeat any of that? Of course not. But now that I've done so much shadow work I can see how there was light in my life as well.

These days, I focus on the light more than the darkness, but when my shadow wants to speak, I listen. When I feel angry (or any other dark emotion) I look at it and see what it's trying to tell me rather than suppressing it or acting on it. If I'm angry it means that something in my life is out of balance. Many times I can fix it and get back on track, and sometimes it's completely out of my hands yet I know that I'll be okay.

You don't need anything special to do this exercise. I've even pulled a pen out of my purse and drew on napkins. It is nice though to have items always ready when you are. When you get out your art media go someplace quiet and turn your attention inwards.

I usually start each session by saying out loud, "Shadow self, what do you want me to know right now?" Or, "Shadow self, what do you want to say right now?" I then just start drawing whatever comes to mind. Sometimes I get images, other times words, and still other times just shapes or squiggles. Even if something doesn't make sense or seems strange, just go with it since it will almost always hold hidden feelings, thoughts, or memories.

One time I decided to use markers and, going with gut instinct, I chose neon pink and green. I let my shadow know it was perfectly okay to come out and say something. I then waited. All I got was three neon pink squiggly lines and some neon green squares and triangles.

At first, I thought I was revisiting the geometric drawing I had mentioned just a moment ago, but this felt different. As I looked over this drawing I felt sad and had a lump in my throat. Where was this all coming from? I let my mind wander and a friend from the past rose to the surface. It was around 1984 and we were decorating T-shirts with 80s neon colors and designs. We had been very close and each had two kids at the time. (Yes, we were very young mothers!)

Suddenly, I didn't hear from her anymore. She stopped calling, stopped answering my phone calls, and one time when I saw her at the store she had an excuse as to why she couldn't get together as we normally had.

Although I'm introverted by nature, her friendship meant a lot to me so I went to her house and asked if everything was okay. She sighed and told me that she had become a Jehovah's Witness and since I wasn't of her same (brand-new-to-her) faith, she didn't feel comfortable being my friend anymore.

I'm very accepting and open to one's beliefs so her deciding to choose this religious path didn't bother me at all, but it bothered her that I wasn't "one of her people" as she put it. I left feeling very sad for having lost a friend when it didn't need to be that way.

Back then I just felt hurt and confused. Now I realize that we're all on our own paths in life and sometimes they suddenly veer away in another direction. I just didn't realize how hurt I felt by the loss of our friendship. And, yes, I'll admit, I was angry. How could she just throw away years of closeness, fun, shoulder-leaning during hard times, and so much more?

But, as I stared at that very 80s-looking day-glow drawing of mine I realized and admitted that not all was lost. I still had the memories and it wasn't right to obliterate them because of my hurt feelings. So there...my shadow got to express itself and finally be heard after all these years and my conscious self was able to find peace in it all.

The main thing to remember when you do this exercise is to keep an open mind and refrain from judging anything that comes out. Also, just sit with your drawing for a while rather than letting your logical mind jump on it and start telling you what it all supposedly means. Be gentle with yourself and receptive. Allow whatever wants to come to the surface to spill out and onto the paper. These feelings, regardless of how difficult, are part of you but they don't need to run and ruin your life.

Exploring Your Shadow Through Tarot

This is the longest section in the book since I believe that tarot cards are so helpful for learning about yourself and how you handle life's struggles and lessons. They help with self-awareness and often uncover a different point of view regarding a problem or situation. They can also clarify past events, and show why the events took place. Another thing they're extremely helpful for is exploring your shadow.

The tarot is rich in symbolism and what you see in the cards for yourself will be different than what someone else sees. Best of all, you don't need to know the traditional meanings of the cards. In fact, I wholeheartedly believe that reading the tarot intuitively is always best and most accurate. I go into this more in detail in my book *Intuitive Tarot – Learn The Tarot Instantly*, but for now let's just get to some easy, interesting, and eye-opening exercises.

Trust me, anyone can do this. All you need is a deck of tarot cards. If you don't have a deck already, one of the most common is the Rider Waite deck. The Morgan Greer deck is one of my favorites, as is the Connolly deck.

If you go with another deck, make sure that there are pictures for each of the 78 cards. You can do a search online to see the cards before you purchase them. Some decks will have detailed major arcana cards, the first 22, and the rest are just represented by a certain number of pentacles, swords, wands, cups. You want to be sure that there's rich symbolism in every single card.

The imagery on the cards speaks directly to your subconscious or to any spirit guides who can give you insight into your shadow side. There are so many colors, situations, characters, and symbols in these decks that can provide you with a detailed look at where you need to heal and how you can do it. The tarot can show you where the problem is, what's blocking you, and what your options for solving it are.

I'll assume that you already have a deck and are comfortable with exploring your cards even deeper. Following are the very exercises I use to do shadow work. Feel free to try them all or choose the one(s) that resonate most with you at this time.

Getting Started

Shadow work can bring up a lot of emotions and memories so make sure you're feeling mentally, physically, and emotionally grounded before doing any of these tarot exercises. It's not a good idea to read the cards when you're feeling overly emotional or if you're feeling physically bad in any way such as being tired, in too much pain, having a headache, a cold, etc.

Also, don't try to do a tarot exercise if you're in a rush. Shadow work takes time and effort. Your goal is to find answers and guidance so rushing through or feeling bad in any way will just make it more difficult to read the cards or have you believing they can't help you at all.

Go someplace quiet where you won't be interrupted for at least fifteen minutes. I like going into my bedroom and closing the door. By doing this, my family knows not to disturb me unless necessary.

Sit on your bed or the floor, take your cards out of the box and shuffle them several times. You can do a Cauldron Shuffle where you place the cards face down on the floor or your bed and stir them up. I highly recommend doing this the first time you take your cards out of the box since this helps to mix them out of order and imbues the cards with your energy.

Afterward, whenever you do a reading, you can shuffle the deck three or four times as with normal playing cards. Usually, I do the Cauldron Shuffle once a month, just to be sure the cards are good and mixed up, and to air them out a bit.

Feel free to light a candle and/or some incense. I also like playing soft meditation music in the background—something soothing and instrumental or nature sounds. It's important to set the atmosphere in a way that makes you feel calm and centered.

Sometimes I'll add essential oils such as lavender or sandalwood to a diffuser or put a dab on my inner wrists. I also like to set a few crystals or stones out either near my candle and incense or right next to my deck of cards. Don't put too much thought or effort into it. Just do whatever feels natural and calming to you. There are many times where I just sit on my bed, pull out my cards, and get to work.

Also, be sure to have a pen and pad of paper or your journal by your side so you can take notes. You don't want to do your shadow work and forget what the cards showed you.

Tarot And Journaling

<u>Freewriting:</u>

With this exercise, while you're shuffling your cards, think about something that's bothering you right now. What obstacle—either a person or situation—is blocking your path to living life as you wish you could? Who or what is creating negativity for you? Where are you struggling? What's the biggest issue you're facing right now? Choose just one of these to focus on.

Once you have this firmly in your mind, stop shuffling the cards and lay the deck in front of you face down. Now, turn over the first card and lay it beside the deck facing up. As you hold your question or situation in mind, look over the card and just start writing in your journal or notebook. How does the card seem to fit in with the issue you're exploring?

One time when I did this exercise I was addressing the issue of why I always felt I wasn't doing enough as a mother. I had always tried my best to put my kids first and foremost in my life, but, of course, there were several times when I fell short. It went deeper than this though. It was a true fear and something I would beat myself up over again and again.

I drew a card and got the Empress reversed. In most decks, it shows a woman sitting outdoors on a chair/throne with a scepter in one hand. In the Morgan Greer deck I often use she's holding a shield in one arm and a large flower in the other. As I looked over the card I felt that the woman represented my mother.

Since the card was reversed she would literally (if in real life) fall out of the chair and the things in her arms would fall out too. To me, the shield represents protection and she never protected my sister and me. The flower represents nurturing and we never got that from her either.

I could go on about all of the things I noticed in the card that pertained to my mother and childhood, but those are a few of the examples. Also, it wasn't anything I didn't already know. I've always had a fear of being anything like my mother and letting my kids down in some way. Although this wasn't anything new to me, it did show just how deep and wide this shadow was. And, it proved to me, once again, how accurate tarot cards are!

One of the last few lines I wrote in my journal when exploring this shadow was, "I'm not my mother. I need to stop judging myself so harshly. I have a wonderful relationship with my girls!" After that session, every time I started questioning myself as a positive role model for my daughters I remembered those words I told myself. That shadow will always be part of me, but rather than allowing it to make me second-guess myself I now use it as a positive reminder that I'm nothing like my mother was.

<u>Asking Questions</u>

If nothing in the card jumps out at you right away or seems to have no correlation to the issue you're focusing on, sit with this card for a moment and ask yourself one or more of the following questions and see what comes up then do some freewriting about it.

- Why does this keep happening in my life?

- What's the real issue here that I'm not seeing?

- If I dig deeper what will I find?

- Am I ignoring something important that will help me heal?

- Where did this issue first enter my life?

Feel free to come up with questions of your own as well. After all, you know yourself and your life better than anyone else does. Go with this and see what you discover or rediscover.

Shadow Work Tarot Spreads

If you want to dive in even deeper you can use tarot spreads to uncover the how's and why's of your shadow traits. Of course, you can create your own tarot spreads to explore your darker side, but the following ones are some of my favorites.

This first spread is great for doing a lot of work in a short amount of time. It will probably take you a while, so be sure to do this when you don't have anything planned for an hour or so. Something I've done in the past is to lay each card out and write them down in my journal. That way, if I get interrupted I can go back to it later and pull those cards out again.

Digging Deep Spread

You can do the entire spread as-is or pick and choose the areas that are most important to you at this time. I've sometimes only chosen one of the entries that seem to resonate most with me, while other times I've done all 10, though typically I'll choose three since this often gets to the heart of the matter and doesn't take up as much time.

First, choose a shadow trait you want to address. This can be an emotion that surfaces at times such as anger or envy, a fear you might have such as not having enough money, a health issue, a childhood memory, or whatever you want and need to work on right now.

You could also just see what comes up in the cards without focusing on anything in particular. I always have faith that the cards and my higher self will show me what I need to work on or what information needs to be brought to the surface.

Once you've decided on your area of exploration choose one, some, or all of the following guidance entries, laying one card face down for each of them.

- This is what I'm not seeing

- This is what I'm hiding from or denying

- This is something that keeps showing up

- This is where I need help

- This is what I project onto others

- This is one source of my pain

- This is what my inner child wants me to know

- This is what/who stands in my way

- This is how I can move forward

- This is what I can ultimately achieve

As you go over each area one by one, turn the card upright. Look at the details and how they can pertain to what you're exploring and working on. In your journal, write down the sentence and card you got then either do freewriting, write a story about the card, or deliberately think things through and write what you feel the card means for you. You could even write your thoughts and feelings down in list form using one or more words to describe what you see and feel in the card.

Be sure to include the date you're doing the reading so you can go back and see how you've changed and grown over time. Also, write down what deck you used if you use more than one as I do.

Choosing One Area

As I look through my journal right now I see an entry I made several months ago. I chose to go with writing a short story about the card.

May 17ᵗʰ, 2021

- "This is what I'm hiding from or denying." 8 of Swords reversed. (Morgan Greer deck.)

The card shows a woman tied up, blindfolded, and with eight swords surrounding her, almost like a prison. She's wearing a red dress.

Since the card is reversed it tells me that this woman's blindfold and bindings will come off. All of the swords (which I feel represent my mental state and things on my mind) will fall away and she'll be free. Her red dress represents fiery passion and perhaps anger as well.

The woman feels she's been suppressed for a long time and is just now freeing herself from everything that has held her captive. She wants to find her passion again and, yes, she feels angry because so much time has been wasted in this false imprisonment of her own mind. But, at least she now sees that there's a way out.

She's been hiding from intense emotions since they scare her because both of her parents had hot tempers which would scare her as a child. So, she learned to bottle up any intense emotion—whether good or bad. Over time though, she wasn't really living and unintentionally created this prison.

It got to where she didn't want to make any move to disrupt life since change was scary too. She also chose to ignore things in life, preferring to turn a blind eye rather than facing the discomfort of constructive confrontation. In her mind, due to her upbringing, if she voiced any feelings that weren't calm and positive there would be an argument and she might be abandoned—either emotionally or physically—by the people she loves.

She's been working on herself though and, as scary as it might be, she's more comfortable with being her authentic self, even if she's upset or overly excited. She still has healing to do, but she's no longer a prisoner of her own mind.

That was a more lengthy entry, but it was so incredibly helpful to discovering what shadow needed to be heard at the time and why. The story I wrote about the woman was, naturally, about myself. Sometimes writing in the third-person helps to distance ourselves from our emotions and memories, allowing us to go deeper than we dare to otherwise.

Flipping through my journal a little more I see this short entry that I did in list fashion:

November 3rd, 2020

- *"This is what I can ultimately achieve." The Magician upright. (Connolly Deck.)*

Strength

Passion

Intense focus

Teaching others

Balance in all areas of life

Stability

Being outdoors more

Stronger aura

Better finances

Creating my future

These are the things that jumped right out to me as I looked over this card. I didn't write down a description of what the card looked like since I can go back and take it out of the deck if I want to look it over again. I just went with my instincts on what I needed to know and see at the time when I did the reading.

Getting Real Spread

This could also be called the "Brutally Honest Spread" because it gets to the heart of the matter without sugar-coating anything. Yes, tarot cards are helpful and uplifting, but they aren't going to lie to us as we so often lie to ourselves.

For example, I'm a recovering perfectionist and have always needed things to be just-so. That's how I felt safe and in control. When I did this spread I got The Tower for "This is how I subconsciously feel". In most decks, it shows a brick tower with fire, lightning, and people jumping from the windows.

Yes, I knew I needed life to be very stable and secure due to my chaotic childhood, but I didn't realize that deep down inside I believed something horrible would happen if I let go of all of the control I fought for. A little dramatic, right? But, when it's become part of your shadow you don't realize how so many things get blown out of proportion because we've ignored it for so long.

I just thought I felt calmer when life went according to plan. That card showed me I had some deep healing to do and also needed to realize that if things didn't go according to my strict schedule or plans nothing detrimental would happen.

As with the other spreads, shuffle the cards and lay one face down for each of the following then turn them over as you address them one by one.

1. This is my current situation.

2. This is how I consciously feel about it.

3. This is how I subconsciously feel about it.

4. This is how it's hurt me.

5. This is how it's helped me.

6. This is the lesson I need to learn.

The One Scary Card

Everyone has an aversion to at least one card in their deck, if not more. And, depending on what's going on in your life at the time, this "scary card" will probably change. Yes, there's the typical fear of the Death card, Devil, Tower, and others, but some go deeper than that. When your subconscious is ready to work on a particular shadow you'll probably find that at least one card will stick out and create feelings of hate, fear, worry, disgust, or dread in you.

Go through your deck and pick out the card you detest the most at this time. Lay it down in front of you, face up, and take a few minutes to look at it. Notice as much in the card as you can. Examine the details, the colors, and imagery. Allow thoughts and emotions to rise to the surface but don't judge anything or squash it down, just breathe through it and go with these sensations.

Get your journal and write down your thoughts and feelings.

- What sticks out to me in this card?

- What feelings does this card rouse in me?

- What words or thoughts come to mind as I look at it?

- How does it pertain to my life right now?

- How does it pertain to my past?

- What do I need to make peace with or let go of?

Years ago I had an aversion to the 9 of Swords card. In the card, a woman is sitting up in bed, her hands over her face, darkness all around, and 9 swords floating over her head. Yes, the imagery alone is a bit scary, but it really pulled at something inside me. When I did this exercise I realized several things:

I had been having trouble with insomnia.

I had been having nightmares.

I had a lot of stress and pressure in my life at that time.

I felt very alone.

I felt very much "in the dark" as to how to fix my life.

I'd been having trouble with anxiety, headaches, and pain in general.

Up to that point, whenever I encountered that card I felt a sense of dread and panic rising in me so I would push it all down. After doing this exercise though I realized exactly why this card bothered me so much. Although things didn't change overnight, by admitting exactly why the card resonated so deeply I was able to face my life and start working on releasing the stress.

If you have a strong aversion to a specific card don't ignore your feelings. There's a reason that this card is trying to get your attention. It's a part of your shadow showing itself to you so you can work on it.

After you write down all the things you notice in the card that bother you or get your attention list some ways you can feel safer and/or start releasing these feelings. Some things are out of our control and we need to release our fears by accepting that we can't control everything. Most of the time though anything negative we feel about a card can be worked through and worked out.

Love and Hate Spread

This isn't much of a spread since, like the last exercise, you'll only be drawing one card, but this time you'll do so at random. After shuffling your deck either pick the top card or one at random within the deck without looking.

Turn it over face-up and just look at the card for a moment. What immediately jumps out at you? What details catch your attention? What thoughts or memories come to you?

After a minute or two of looking at the card, ask yourself the following questions and answer them in your journal or just think about it. I prefer writing in my journal since I like having something I can come back to in the future to see how I was feeling and if anything has changed.

- What don't I like about this card?

- What do I like about this card?

- What type of energy does the card give off?

- How do both the good and bad aspects of this card pertain to me?

- How can I embody more of the positive and release the negative aspects of this?

One card I have both loved and hated is the 6 of Pentacles. This card typically shows a man standing with six gold coins around him. He's handing gold coins to people who have their hands reaching up to him. In his other hand, he's holding an old-fashioned set of scales.

What I love about this card is the energy of generosity. I imagine myself as the man helping people he cares about because he's doing well financially. He's happy and eager to share his wealth.

What I hate about the card is the energy of desperation or greed. When I imagine myself as the man with money, I see people (who aren't close family members) asking for my financial help. They're taking advantage of me but I'm too nice to say no. Yes, this has happened to me more than once, but I've since learned from this shadow!

I also see those outstretched hands asking for money as myself in the past when I was very poor. I was on public assistance and, to me, the man on the card represented the government. I always felt so bad about myself when I struggled financially.

Over time I've learned to say no when I can't afford to help others out—whether it's with my time or money. Sure, I've lost a couple of friends over this, but I'm not a personal ATM and I can't overextend myself when I have my own life to tend to. I've also learned to not feel bad about myself for having needed to be on public assistance. In truth, I was grateful for the help when I needed it.

What will you learn about your love/hate relationship with a certain card?

Things Are Good Spread

When doing shadow work we tend to focus on a lot of what we perceive as negative. Those dark feelings and reactions, those tough things we tend to ignore, refusing to look them in the eye. In this spread though we're going to focus on what's going well in your life. No matter how bad things seem to be and no matter how long you feel you've been on this negative path there is *always* some good.

In my own experience, and seeing this with friends and clients, I've found that the more positive we can see in our lives the stronger we become. We can then more easily work on our shadows and become whole again.

Lay out four cards face down after shuffling your deck. The cards will represent:

- What is going well in my life as a whole?

- Why is it going well for me personally?

- How is this helping me?

- How can I improve this even more?

Even if the cards you draw seem to make no sense, just sit with them a bit and see what comes to you. One time when I did this the first card I got was the Devil. I thought to myself, "What? How does this point to something going well in my life when it seems so bad and negative?"

Rather than thinking that I wasn't in the right frame of mind to do shadow work this day I tried to see the positive in this card. This card typically shows a devil figure with two people in chains. Sounds bad, doesn't it? But, I was determined to find the good in it!

Something that was going well in my life was that I felt I had conquered a couple of issues that had bothered me for decades. One was my finances and one was releasing a deep-down need to be in a relationship "no matter what". For far too long I felt that to be whole I needed to be with a partner. In reality, my wholeness was found when I gave myself time to be single and do a lot of shadow work. So, the two people in chains represented *me* gaining control of two things that used to control me.

Reaching Your Goals Spread

This spread can help you discover what you truly want to accomplish—regardless of what your conscious mind thinks it wants—and how to get there. As always, shuffle your deck and for this spread lay out three cards face down. These will represent:

- What is my true goal right now?

- What's blocking me from achieving it?

- What do I need to do to meet this goal?

When I did this spread one time the issue seemed so small and I couldn't believe it had anything to do with shadow work. However, I went with it so I could discover what my subconscious had to say.

The first card I drew was the 4 of Cups upright. This card typically speaks about boredom, waiting for an opportunity, and so forth. But what caught my eye most was the woman in the card who was outside with lush greenery all around, sitting against the trunk of a tree. The whole scene felt so relaxed and peaceful. I admitted to myself that I wanted to be outside in nature a lot more. That's where I feel calm and at one with the world.

The next card I drew was the Queen of Swords. This is what was blocking me from achieving it. I saw myself as the woman in the card. She seemed so focused on using her sword that she had little time for anything else. To me, this represented how I often become a workaholic. The woman needed to put her sword down and enjoy some time to relax!

For the final card, I got The Chariot. In the card, a man is holding the reins of two horses who are pulling his vehicle. He looks focused, but in a calm way. One horse is white and the other is black. I could see how this was telling me that, to achieve my goal of being out in nature and relaxing, I needed far more balance in life. I needed control over myself so I could get work done but I also needed to spend time doing whatever made me feel happy and calm.

When doing shadow work with tarot cards, most of the time they're going to tell you what you already know, but that's the beauty in it. One, if you *are* seeing things you already know about yourself then you know that the cards are in sync with your energy and subconscious. Two, it's a reminder that if this is coming up again then you haven't completely worked through it.

And, yes, there are times when you learn something totally new about yourself. So new in fact that it's easy to dismiss. The card(s) came up for a reason though. Be fearless, dive right in, and see what you can learn.

Shadow work is an ongoing process, but the rewards are endless. In the beginning, you might choose to do shadow work daily, then less often as you heal, become stronger, more confident, and successful. Always look at your shadow as an opportunity to learn more about yourself rather than something you want to exorcise from your life.

I highly recommend trying each of the above spreads at least once. Afterward, you'll most likely have your favorites that you go to again and again. Others, although greatly helpful, might have to be explored when you're in the right frame of mind.

Always feel free to personalize the spreads so they work better for you and your circumstances. There are times when I choose just one card to answer a whole list of questions. After all, the symbolism is so rich and detailed you could write an entire book about each one! At other times I've laid out three cards for each question and I've also created many of my own spreads at the spur of the moment.

Daily Card

Even if you don't feel like doing a complete spread or if you don't have anything in particular you want to explore, something I've found helpful is to pull a card out of the deck at random and ask, "What do I need to know right now?" I typically do this every morning, just to get an idea of what I need to keep in mind, explore, or heal.

You don't even need to look that deeply into it or write about it. I usually set the card on my dresser and go about my day. Before going to bed I look at the card and see if anything about it pertains to what I encountered since waking up. It's a good way to keep in touch with your subconscious. After all, you're partners in this life and need to work together.

Whichever exercise you use, always end the session by thanking your higher self, inner child, and your guides. I usually close my eyes, put my palms together at heart level, take a few cleansing breaths, smile, then say "thank you for your help and guidance".

Shadow work is a lifelong process. I've found it incredibly helpful to go back over my journals to see where I've changed and grown and how things have shifted in my life. In my older journals, I've noticed that there was a lot of anger and fear in them, and a huge hatred of change—even positive change.

As the years have passed those shadow traits still exist within me but to a much lesser degree. Now when they rise to the surface I can almost always stop myself before reacting to those feelings and ask my shadow what it wants me to know.

When The Cards Don't Make Sense

There are times when I'm reading for myself and the cards just aren't talking. Nothing makes sense, no matter how long I sit and stare at them. Nothing resonates and my mind is a complete blank.

Rather than forcing the issue, I know that I'm not in the right frame of mind at the moment to do any shadow work. I might have too much "real life" floating around in my head or I might not be ready to work on a particular issue just yet. If we aren't ready we won't understand the cards. We won't see the information we need to heal, even though it's right there in front of our eyes.

I don't like thinking about the many times I stressed myself out trying to turn all the gibberish I was seeing into something useful. I'd get upset with myself, wondering what was wrong with me, and doubting that the cards could help me at all. Yeah, my mind tends to go a bit overboard at times.

Nowadays, if nothing is clicking I'll shuffle the cards, put them back in their box, and try again later or the following day. "When the student is ready the teacher appears."

On the other hand, if the cards are giving you answers that make sense *and* you feel the guidance is constructive and positive, then you know it's a good time to do shadow work.

Don't Give Up

Shadow work can be difficult and it often seems like a never-ending journey. There will be times when you feel exhausted, when you cry, want to scream, and want to give up. I promise you, it gets better and easier over time. Your shadow has either been locked up or given free rein for so long that in the beginning, it can be pretty rough. It's like going to the first few sessions of therapy where everything spills out and overwhelms you.

I've read books and articles and even heard some people mention that shadow work doesn't have to be hard and can be instantaneous. They claim that you can heal within minutes of discovering or facing a shadow trait. I believe, and have experienced both personally and professionally, that this isn't the truth. *If it's easy then you aren't doing it right or going deep enough.*

As we talked about before, even the smallest cut you get still needs attention. The deeper the wound the more attention it needs and the longer it will take for it to heal. And, yes, sometimes you're left with scars. How are emotional wounds any different? Just as we can learn to love our physical scars that are a testament to what's happened in our lives, so, too, are our shadow scars.

If you ignore your darker side it will eventually own you and run your life. It will ruin relationships, block your way to any success you're striving for, and put a stop to anything positive you try to accomplish.

Shadow work takes courage because you'll be facing your inner demons, all the pain of your past, and the deepest, darkest parts of yourself. At the very least, it can be difficult to acknowledge that you possess traits that you detest in others.

When you're really truthful though you'll uncover layer after layer of your personality and will eventually become whole again. The real you! The perfectly imperfect person you're meant to be. This happens when you own your shadow and use it as a partner and ally rather than avoiding it or repressing it. This soul-deep work is what has changed my life more than anything because it gets to the very core of our issues instead of focusing on superficial symptoms.

Shadow work has been the most important journey I've embarked on. It's helped me to uncover old wounds, let go of outworn beliefs, heal from childhood traumas, and realized everything I had been projecting outwards.

My shadow has helped me to see things more clearly, has helped me to understand others and myself better, and shown me how to accept all that I am. In doing so, I've found an inner peace that I never believed existed.

It might seem like everything in the shadow self is dark and ugly, but I guarantee you'll find some helpful, interesting, and even beautiful things buried there as well. You might uncover dreams and goals you haven't thought about for years or had given up on long ago. And, yes, you'll find some painful or shocking things as well. It's all part of the process.

It's also easy to see all of these painful parts as only negative, but everything has two sides to it. Rather than ignoring all the stuff that's been shoved down in there throughout the years, take each one out, hold it up to the light, and see what it can teach you.

Contact Me/Book A Reading

Whether your problems or concerns are in the areas of love, finances, family, career, health, education, or your path in life, I offer professional intuitive counseling, caring guidance, and solutions that work!

I'll let you know absolutely everything that comes through in the reading which typically includes past, present, and future energies, guidance, time frames and predictions. Each reading is in-depth, filled with positive energy and guidance, and includes one free clarification email.

All readings are done via email. By offering my readings through email you'll be able to save your reading and go back to it again and again for guidance.

I look forward to reading for you!

Check out my readings, books, blog posts, and more on my website:

DrKellyPsychic.com

Or email me directly at: DrKellyPsychicCounselor@gmail.com